LESSON 1

NEW LETTERS AND VOWELS:

◌ֵ	ב	בּ
AY	V	B

T0151868

1. Here are the two Hebrew letters you've learned: BET בּ & VET ב

2. Write the letter with the saying sound of B _____.

3. Write the letter with the saying sound of V _____.

4. Whenever you see this letter בּ you sound it _____.

5. Whenever you see this letter ב you sound it _____.

6. The vowel AY as in DAY is written _____.

7. To read the sound BAY, we combine the BET בּ and the vowel

   AY as in DAY ◌ֵ so: בֵּ

   Practice writing a whole row of בֵּ beginning here

   _____ _____ _____ _____ _____ _____ _____ _____ _____ _____ _____

   Now do a row with the sound of VAY.

   _____ _____ _____ _____ _____ _____ _____ _____ _____ _____ _____

8. Read this line aloud, slowly at first, then try it increasing your speed with each reading. (When there is no vowel just give the saying sound of the letter.)

   בֵּ בֵּ בּ בֵּ ב בֵּ בֵּ ב בּ בֵּ בֵּ בֵּ

LESSON 2

NEW LETTERS AND VOWELS:

AH AH D R

LETTERS AND VOWELS YOU KNOW:

AY B V

---

1. This ר is RAYSH. This ד is DAHLET. Under each letter below write its saying sound.

ר ר ר ד ר ד ר ד ד

_____ _____ _____ _____ _____ _____ _____ _____ _____

2. We'll combine the ר and ד with the vowel ֵ AY. You fill in the sounds.

(Remember when you use English letters, always write them in the order you are accustomed to: DAY and RAY.)

_____ _____ _____ _____ _____ _____

3. Now we'll combine the new vowels ַ and ָ AH as in OOMPAH.

   a. This letter and vowel בֵ are read as _____.

   b. This letter and vowel בָ are read as _____.

   c. This letter and vowel רָ are read as _____.

   d. This letter and vowel דַ are read as _____.

4. Match these two columns.

RAY ( )	(1) בֵ
BAH ( )	(2) בָ
DAY ( )	(3) רֵ
VAH ( )	(4) דַ

5. Let's try combining and reading two syllables.

This reads RAH RAH רָ רַ ←

This reads _____ רַבָּ ←

This reads _____ דַבָּ ←

6. One of these sounds reads VAH BAY. Which one? ( )

דַבָּ רַבָּ בַּר רַב דַבָּ ←

(e) (d) (c) (b) (a)

7. The sounds BAY RAH are written _____ _____ ←
(1) (2) (use ־) (2) (1)

The sounds DAH BAH are written _____ _____
(1) (2) (use both vowels) (2) (1)

The sounds VAY DAH are written _____ _____
(1) (2) (use either vowel) (2) (1)

8. Try to read these now, speedily but accurately.

בַּבַ בָּדָ דַרַ רָב דָבַ בַּרַ ←

(Have someone 'time' your reading when you know it well.)

9. You know that to make a Hebrew word we combine syllables and read them together. Here are three Hebrew words.

a. The word רָב reads_____.

b. The word בַּר reads_____.

c. The word דַבָּר reads_____.

LESSON 3

NEW LETTERS:

S SH

LETTERS AND VOWELS YOU KNOW:

AH AH AY D R V B

1. SHEEN is written this way_____.

2. SEEN is written this way_____.

3. To read the sound SAY, we add the vowel AY .. to the  so: 

   Write a line of  beginning here _____

   _____

   Now try SHAY  _____

   _____

   How about a row of SAH _____

   _____

4. Fill in the correct vowel to complete each sound.

   SAY SHAH SAH SHAY

   (use other vowel) (either vowel)

5. Ready for some practice reading aloud? But no mistakes, please; remember accuracy is most important.

   Try it again doing it more quickly.

6. We'll try two syllables now. See how quickly you can read these.

שֶׁשֶׁ שָׁשֶׁ שֶׁשָׁ שֶׁשֶׁ שָׁשֶׁ ←

(Bit of a tongue-twister, wasn't it?)

7. These are the letters you know. We'll write their saying sounds, you write their names.

Saying Sounds	V	R	S	B	D	SH
	ב	ר	ס	בּ	ד	שׁ

Names _____ _____ _____ _____ _____ _____

8. Under each letter and vowel write its sound.

בָּ שֶׁ שֵׁ רֶ ←

_____ _____ _____ _____

9. Now write the sounds of each of these syllables.

שֵׁב בָּד רֶשׁ שֹׁר ←

_____ _____ _____ _____

שֹׁר שָׁבַ שֵׁד

_____ _____ _____

10. Shall we try some speed-reading again?

בַּ דֶ דָ בֶּ שָׁ שַׁ רֶ בַּ דַ ←

11. Practice reading double syllables now.

דַבַּ שָׁדָ רֶשָׁ שַׁבַּ שֹׁרָ ←

You've learned six letters and three vowels. See how quickly you can read them. And more than that, see how well you can read the Hebrew words at the bottom of the page.

1	בּ	בּ	ב	בּ	ב	ב	ב	בּ	ב	בּ	ב	בּ
2	ר	ד	ד	ד	ר	ד	ר	ר	ד	ר	ר	ר
3	שׁ	שׁ	שׁ	שׁ	שׁ	שׁ	שׁ	שׁ	שׁ	שׁ	שׁ	שׁ
4	בּ	שׁ	ר	שׁ	ד	ב	ר	ב	שׁ	בּ	ד	שׁ
5	־	־	־	־	־	־	־	־	־	־	־	־
6	דָ	בָּ	רָ	שָׁ	בַ	שַׁ	שֵׁ	בֵ	דֵ	שֵׁ	רֵ	בֵּ
7	שַׁבָּ	שַׁב	רָבַ	רָב	שָׁרַ	שָׁר						
8	דַבֵּ	דַב	שַׁרַ	שַׁר	שָׁרֵ	שָׁשׁ						
9	דַבֵּר	רֵשׁ	שֵׁב	בָּשָׂר								
	speak!	"R"	sit!	meat								
10	דָרַשׁ	שָׁבַר	שֵׁשׁ	בָּרָד								
	explained	broke	six	hail								

LESSON 4

NEW LETTERS:

ת תּ

T T

LETTERS YOU KNOW:

ש שׁ ד ר ב בּ

S SH D R V B

VOWELS YOU KNOW:

ַ ָ ֵ

AH AH AY

---

1. TAHV is written תּ and has the saying sound of _____.

2. TAHV also is written this way ת and still has the saying sound of _____.

3. The three vowels you've learned are:

   ֵ AY as in _____

   ָ AH as in _____

   ַ AH as in _____

4. Practice reading these vowels aloud, beginning here

   ַ ֵ ַ ָ ֵ ַ ֵ ָ ָ ַ

5. Now read these vowels combined with this תּ TAHV and this ת TAHV.

   תֵ תֵּ תָ תַ תָּ תַּ תֵ תָ תַּ

6. Under each Hebrew letter below, write its name.

   ר בּ תּ שׁ

   _____ _____ _____ _____

7. This time we'll give you the name of each letter, you write the Hebrew letter.

   TAHV SEEN DAHLET VET

   _____ _____ _____ _____

8. This letter and vowel שָׁ reads _____.

9. This letter and vowel תֶ reads _____.

10. This letter and vowel תַ reads _____.

11. This letter and vowel תָ reads _____.

12. Match these columns.

TAY ( )	(1) תָ
TAH ( )	(2) תַ
VAH ( )	(3) תֶ
SAH ( )	(4) שָׁ

13. Practice reading aloud each of these syllables.

שָׁ בָּ תֶ בַ דָ בָ רַ בֶ ←

14. Read these phrases slowly the first time. Then read them again increasing your speed. But remember accuracy is more important than speed.

שָׁבָ שַׁבָּ תֶבַ בַּת רָשָׁ דָרַ ←

15. Here are several Hebrew words. One of them reads SHAH-BAHT—SABBATH. Copy that word in the space provided.

שָׁר בַּת דָּבָר שַׁבָּת ←

This is the word for SABBATH _____.

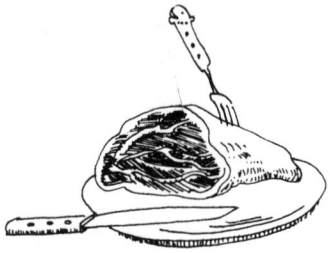

Here's a review of all the letters and vowels you know. Say out loud the name of each letter in the first four rows. Then continue to read. See if you can find the Hebrew word for SABBATH.

1	בּ	תּ	בּ	תּ	ב	תּ	בּ	ת	ב	תּ	בּ	ת
2	שׂ	שׂ	שׂ	שׂ	שׂ	שׂ	שׂ	שׂ	שׂ	שׂ	שׂ	שׂ
3	ר	ר	ד	ר	ד	ד	ד	ד	ר	ד	ר	ר
4	תּ	ת	שׂ	ר	תּ	בּ	ת	שׂ	ד	ב	ת	תּ
5	ד	־	ד	־	ד	־	ד	־	ד	־	ד	־
6	תָּ	תֵּ	תַ	תָּ	תַ	תֵּ	תֵ	תָּ	תַ	תֵּ	תֵ	תֵ
7	בָּ	תַּ	שֵׁ	רָ	דֵ	שֵׁ	בֵ	תָּ	בַּ	תֵּ	דַ	רֵ
8	שָׁבַ	שַׁבָּ	רָתָ	תֵּשַׁ	דָבָ	בָּשָׂ	שָׁרֵ					
9	שֵׁת	שָׂרֵת	שָׂשׂ	שָׁת	שַׁבָּת							
	Seth	service	glad	put	Sabbath							
10	דַת	בַּת	רַבַּת	רָתָת	בָּשָׂר							
	religion	daughter	many (poetic form)	to tremble	meat							

LESSON 5

NEW LETTERS:

מ ל

M L

LETTERS YOU KNOW:

ת תּ שׂ שׁ ד ר ב בּ

T T S SH D R V B

VOWELS YOU KNOW:

ַ ָ ֶ

AH AH AY

---

1. The LAHMED starts above the line so: ל
   Write a row of 12 LAHMEDs beginning here _____

_____ _____ _____ _____ _____ _____ _____ _____ _____ _____ _____ _____

_____ _____ _____ _____ _____ _____ _____ _____ _____ _____ _____ _____

   Add the vowel AH ָ to the first 4 LAHMEDs.

   Add this vowel AH ַ to the next 4 LAHMEDs.

   Add the vowel AY ֶ to the last 4 LAHMEDs.

2. Now read aloud the row of letters and vowels you've just written.

3. Try it again to gain more speed.

4. Read these syllables:

		Now write their sounds.	
לָ (2)	לַ (1)	_____ (2)	_____ (1)
לַ (2)	לֶ (1)	_____ (2)	_____ (1)
לֶ (2)	לָ (1)	_____ (2)	_____ (1)

5. Here is the MEM מ with the saying sound of _____.

6. Next to each MEM מ and vowel write its sound.

   This syllable מַ reads _____

   This syllable מֶ reads _____

   This syllable מָ reads _____

7. Which sounds in this row read MAH MAH? Put a star over them.

   לָל לָמָ מָמָ לֶמַ מַמַ לָל

8. Let's practice some reading aloud. We'll include all the letters you know. Do it slowly the first time. Then repeat it, increasing your speed with each reading.

   בֶּ לַ בָּ מֶ שָׁ תַ רָ דֶ שַׁ תֶ

   (If you had any difficulty remembering Hebrew letters or vowels, refer to the top of the page at the beginning of this Lesson.)

9. Now try speed-reading two syllables aloud.

   שָׁמַ לֶבָ תָּרַ תַדֶ שָׁבָ בַּמֶ

10. You know how we write the word for heart, LAY-V. We use the LAHMED ל, the vowel AY ֶ and the VET ב, so: לֶב. Now you write it the _____ way it is sometimes written: LAY-VAH-V. _____

11. Fill in the correct vowels to make this word read LAH-MAH-D. למד

12. And make this word read LAH-VAH-SH. לבש

13. This word מַר reads MAHR.

    You write the word SHAH-MAHR. _____

Can you find the first word in BAR MITZVAH below?
How about the first word in BAT MITZVAH?

1 בּ ב ר ד שׁ שׂ ל מ תּ ת ־ ד ־

2 בְּ בַ רָ דַ שֶׁ שַׂ לָ מֵ תְּ תָ

3 רַבַּ שַׁבָּ דָבָ בָּר לָמַ מָשָׁ

4	בַּר	שָׂר	שַׂר	מַר	תָּמָר
	son	sings	leader	Mr.	date
5	שֵׁשׁ	שֵׁב	שֵׁת	לָתֵת	שָׁרֵת
	six	sit!	Seth	to give	service
6	בַּת	דַּת	שָׂת	רַבַּת	שַׁבָּת
	daughter	religion	put	many	Sabbath
7	רַב	בָּד	שָׁב	שָׂשׂ	רֵשׁ
	rabbi	linen	returned	glad	"R"
8	דָּבָר	שָׁבַר	שָׁמַר	שַׁמָּשׁ	
	thing	broke	guarded	attendant	
9	לָבַשׁ	לֵבָב	בַּלֵּבָב	לָמַד	
	wore	heart	in the heart	studied	
10	מָשָׁל	בָּרַד	דָּרַשׁ	דַּבֵּר	
	proverb	hail	explained	speak!	

LESSON 6

NEW VOWELS:

וּ	וֹ
OO	O

NEW LETTER:

ם

FINAL M

LETTERS YOU KNOW:

ל	מ	ת	תּ	שׂ	שׁ	ד	ר	ב	בּ
L	M	T	T	S	SH	D	R	V	B

VOWELS YOU KNOW:

ָ	ַ	ֵ
AH	AH	AY

---

1. Let's have a quiz to see how many letters you can identify. Next to each letter write its saying sound.

f. _____ ל

g. _____ ד

h. _____ ת

i. _____ ר

j. _____ שׂ

a. _____ שׁ

b. _____ מ

c. _____ בּ

d. _____ תּ

e. _____ ב

(Check your answers at the top of the page.)

2. This will be more difficult. We'll give you their names, you write the correct Hebrew letter next to each one. Ready?

f. RAYSH _____

g. TAHV _____

h. SHEEN _____

i. BET _____

a. MEM _____

b. LAHMED _____

c. DAHLET _____

d. SEEN _____

e. VET _____

3. When we say that a letter is a FINAL LETTER you know that it is used only at the

_____ of a word. This letter ם used only at the end of a word is

_____ MEM.

4. After each syllable in this row, add the FINAL MEM

___בָּ ___דָ ___תַ ___שֵׁ ___לַ

5. Read the phrases you've just written. Then re-read them more speedily. Remember accuracy first, then speed.

6. Here are the two new vowels: O as in NO וֹ and OO as in FOOD וּ.
Write the sounds under each of these letters combined with the vowel O

מוֹ לוֹ שׁוֹ תוֹ דוֹ

_____ _____ _____ _____ _____

7. Now let's add the FINAL MEM and read these syllables:

דוֹם תוֹם שׁוֹם לוֹם מוֹם

8. Practice reading aloud the vowel OO וּ now.

מוּמוּ תוּתוּ לוּלוּ שׁוּשׁוּ

9. Read each of these words aloud carefully, then draw a circle around the one that reads SHAH-M.

שֵׁם שָׁלֵם שָׁם שָׁם

10. This word דוֹר reads DOR.

Add the vowels that will make this word read DOROT. ד ר ת

11. Remember this word? שָׁלוֹם

It reads _____.

12. Write the Hebrew words for SHAH-BAHT SHAH-LOM.

_____

Look for some Hebrew words here that are connected with special Jewish holidays. Can you find them?

1 וֹ וּ וּ וֹ ־ וּ ־ וֹ ־ ־ ־ וּ וֹ ־

2 ל ם מ מ ל ם מ ל ם ל

3 לוֹמֵ לָמַ שוֹמֵ שָׁמַ לוֹבֵ לָבַ

4 מָרוֹ דָרוֹ שָׁלוֹ שָׁלֹ שָׁלֵ בַּלֵ

5 בָּרוּ מַבּוּ תּוֹרָ לוֹם לֵם רוֹם

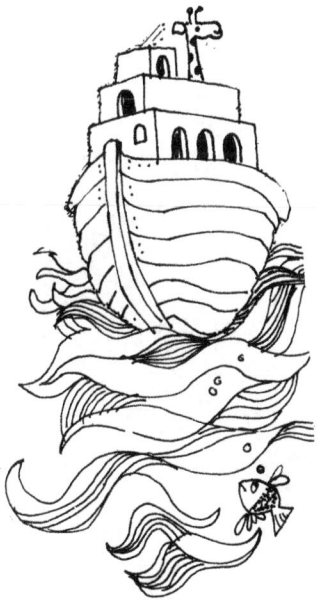

6 מוֹשָׁב מָרוֹר מַבּוּל לוּלָב

settlement bitter herbs flood lulav

7 לוֹמֵד לָמַד לוֹבֵשׁ לָבַשׁ

studies studied wears wore

8 שָׁם שָׂם דָּם רָם מָרוֹם דָּרוֹם מַר

there puts blood high high place south Mr.

9 שַׁבָּת שָׁלוֹם שָׁלֵם שַׁמָּשׁ שֵׁם

Sabbath greetings whole attendant name

10 דוֹד דוֹר בָּרוּר שָׁלֹשׁ תּוֹרָתוֹ

uncle generation clear three His Torah

LESSON 7

NEW LETTERS:

FINAL N	V	Y

LETTERS YOU KNOW:

S	SH	D	R	V	B

FINAL M	L	M	T	T

VOWELS:

OO	O	AH	AH	AY

---

1. Here is the smallest letter in the Hebrew alphabet . Its name is YUD and its saying sound is _____.

2. Add the correct vowel to each YUD to complete the sound required.

_____	_____	_____	_____	_____
YAH	YOO	YAY	YAH	YO

3. Read over the sounds you've completed above.

   a. Now cover the English letters and read the syllables again. Check your answer to be sure you're reading it correctly.

   b. Try speed-reading the line this time.

4. Match these two columns.

YOO	( )	(1)	
YAH	( )	(2)	
YO	( )	(3)	
YAY	( )	(4)	

5. One of these words reads YOM as in YOM KIPPUR. Which one? ( )

(c)	(b)	(a)

6. Even though VAHV ו and VET ב have the same saying sound you know that they are two different letters.

   Both ו and ב have the saying sound of _____.

7. Under each syllable write its sound.

   וֹ וָ בוּ בוֹ וֶ

   _____ _____ _____ _____ _____

8. Next to each of these letters and vowels write the sound.

   This syllable בָ reads _____.

   This syllable וֹ reads _____.

   This syllable וֶ reads _____.

   This syllable בוֹ reads _____.

9. בָ is called _____ and has the saying sound of _____.

   ו is called _____ and has the saying sound of _____.

   ן is called FINAL NUN and has the saying sound of _____.

10. Because it is used only at the end of a word ן is called _____ _____.

11. Combined with the BET ב, the SHEEN שׁ, and the TAHV ת, here are three words ending with the FINAL NUN.
    Under each one write its sound.

    תֶן שֵׁן בֵּן

    _____ _____ _____

12. Using YUD, VAHV and FINAL NUN, write the Hebrew word for "Greek," YAH-VAH-N. (use this vowel ָ AH)

    _____ ←

Sometimes people confuse the י, the ו, and the final ן. Be sure you don't.

1 יִ יַ יָ יִ יוֹ יַ יוֹ יָ יוֹ יוּ

2 וְ וַ וֶ וִ וּ וֹ וַ ווֹ וָ וּ וֵ

3 שָׁן שֵׁן וָן בָּן שׁוֹן לוֹן

4 תַּיָ דַיָ דַיֵ בַּיָ בָּיוֹ לַיָ לַיוֹ

5 יוֹרֵ יָרַ יוֹתֵ יָן יוֹשֵׁ יָשַׁ יוֹמָ

6	יוֹרֵד	יָרַד	יוֹרֵשׁ	יָרַשׁ	יוֹתֵר
	goes down	went down	heir	inherited	more
7	יָם	יוֹם	בַּיּוֹם	יֵשׁ	בֵּין	בֵּית
	sea	day	on the day	there is	between	house of
8	יוֹשֵׁב	יָשַׁב	יָשׁוּב	תַּיָר	וָו
	sits	sat	will return	tourist	hook
9	יָשָׁן	יָשָׁר	יָשֵׁן	שֵׁן	מָלוֹן
	old	straight, honest	sleeps	tooth	hotel
10	דַּיָן	מַתָּן	מוּבָן	לָשׁוֹן	יָד
	judge	gift	meaning	language	hand

LESSON 8

NEW VOWEL—SILENT: ְ

NEW LETTERS— SILENT: ע א

LETTERS YOU KNOW:

ם	ל	מ	ת	תּ	שׂ	שׁ	ד	ר	ב	בּ
FINAL M	L	M	T	T	S	SH	D	R	V	B

VOWELS:

ֹ	ֹ	ַ	ָ	ֶ			ן	ו	י
OO	O	AH	AH	AY			FINAL N	V	Y

---

1. AHLEF א and AHYIN ע are the two SILENT LETTERS. Write the letter called for.

_____	_____	_____	_____	_____	_____	_____
AHLEF	AHLEF	AHYIN	AHLEF	AHYIN	AHYIN	AHLEF

2. We've written the letters this time. You add the correct vowels. Don't let the O and OO fool you.

א	ע	ע	א	ע	א	א	ע	א
OO	AH	AY	OO	AH	O	AH	O	AY

(Check your answers at the top of the page.)

3. Read the sounds you've just completed in the row above. Is your speed improving? Cover the English sounds and read the row again.

4. Here are the א and ע combined with vowels plus the FINAL NUN ן or FINAL MEM ם. Fill in the sounds under each one.

עֵן	אֵם	אוֹם	אָן	עַם
_____	_____	_____	_____	_____

5. Now fill in these sounds.

עַל	עֵת	אֵל	אַת	אוֹר	עַד
_____	_____	_____	_____	_____	_____

6. Remember what you learned about the vowel O? In most cases it is written this way וֹ . Sometimes it appears only as a dot ּ over a letter.

Can you read this word? רֹאׁש

The saying sound of the first letter ר is _____.

The vowel ּ is _____.

The saying sound of the next letter א is _____.

The saying sound of the last letter ׁש is _____.

The word רֹאׁש reads _____.

7. Now try this one: עוֹלָם

The saying sound of the first letter ע is _____.

The vowel וֹ is _____.

The saying sound of the next letter ל is _____.

The next vowel ָ is _____.

The saying sound of the last letter ם is _____.

When you see the word עוֹלָם you read it _____. It means "universe," or "world."

8. The silent vowel ְ SHVAH is written under a Hebrew letter.

It has _____ sound.

9. Write the SHVAH under each of these letters.

DAHLET	SHEEN	LAHMED	BET	VAHV
ד	שׁ	ל	ב	ו

10. Practice reading the sounds you've just completed. Now cover the names above each letter. Do you recognize the letters? Know what to do if you don't recognize each letter?

This time there are two reading drill sheets, with many words you'll find in prayers. See how many you recognize. Have you noticed how many numbers have been included? Do you remember how to say NINE, FOUR, THREE, SIX?

1 אַ אָ אוֹ אֵ אוּ אוֹ אֵ אוּ

2 עוּ עַ עוֹ עֵ עוּ עוֹ עָ עֵ עוֹ

3 א ע ע ע א ע א ע א ע ע א ע

4 בְּ דוֹ עַ שוּ תְּ יוֹ אֵ לְ עוּ

5 עַם אֵם לֹא אֵין עַל אָב

6 אָבוֹ מָבוֹ אָרוֹ אָדֹ אַבָּא

7 שָׁאַ שַׁעַ עָמַ אָמַ אֲבָל

8 עוֹבֵ מוֹעֵ אוֹמֵ שׁוֹאֵ אֵשׁ

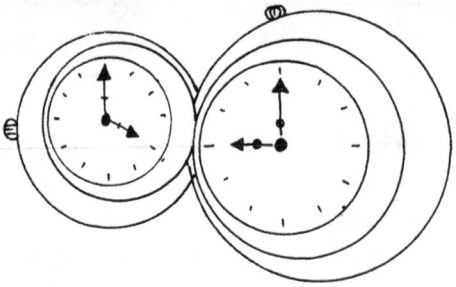

1	אָבוֹת	אָרוֹן	אָדוֹן	מָבוֹא
	fathers	ark	Mr., sir	introduction
2	יוֹדֵעַ	יָדַע	לָדַעַת	מַדוּעַ
	knows	knew	to know	why
3	אוֹמֵר	אָמַר	שׁוֹאֵל	שָׁאַל
	says	said	asks	asked
4	עוֹבֵד	עָבַד	לַעֲבֹד	לַעֲשׂוֹת
	works	worked	to work	to do
5	עוֹמֵד	עָמַד	לַעֲמֹד	שָׂשׂוֹן
	stands	stood	to stand	rejoicing
6	שׁוֹמֵעַ	שָׁמַע	שְׁמַע	שָׁבוּעַ	שָׁבוּעוֹת
	hears	hear!	week	weeks, Festival of Weeks
7	עַמּוֹ	לְעַמּוֹ	מְאֹד	לְמַעַן
	his people	to his people	very	for the sake of
8	בְּתֵאָבוֹן	תֵּשַׁע	אַרְבַּע	שָׁעוֹן
	good appetite!	nine	four	clock

LESSON 9

NEW LETTERS:

גּ	נ
G	N

LETTERS YOU KNOW:

ת	תּ	שׂ	שׁ	ד	ר	ב	בּ
T	T	S	SH	D	R	V	B

ע	א	ן	ו	י	ם	ל	מ
SILENT	FINAL N	V	Y	FINAL M	L	M	

VOWELS YOU KNOW:

ְ	ֹ	ֹ	ַ	ַ	ֵ
SILENT	OO	O	AH	AH	AY

---

1. The regular NUN used at the beginning or middle of a word is written נ .

   This letter ן used only at the end of a word is _____ _____

2. NUN is written _____ . GIMEL is written _____.

3. Here is a row of NUNs and GIMELs. Under each letter write its saying sound.

   גּ נ נ גּ נ גּ נ גּ גּ

   _____ _____ _____ _____ _____ _____ _____ _____ _____ ←

4. Now we'll add vowels to the נ and גּ . Under each syllable fill in its sound.

   גּוֹגּוֹ גּוֹנוֹ נוֹ נֵ גּֽ

   _____ _____ _____ _____ _____ _____ ←

5. Practice reading the line above.

   a. Cover the English sounds and read the line again.
   b. Are you able to read it accurately as well as speedily?

6. Practice reading these sounds you know with the FINAL NUN ן added.

   גַן נָן נוֹן נוֹן גֵן נֵן

7. Below are letters you know. We've given their names, you supply their saying sounds.

AHLEF	MEM	TAHV	SHEEN	RAYSH	YUD	VAHV
א	מ	ת	שׁ	ר	י	ו
_____	_____	_____	_____	_____	_____	_____

8. Fill in the correct vowels to complete these sounds:

LAY	NOO	B	GO	AH	YO	SHAY
ל	נ	בּ	ג	ע	י	שׁ
_____	_____	_____	_____	_____	_____	_____

9. The Hebrew ending נוּ on a word usually means "our." It is used very often. Let's practice reading it.

The word אָנוּ is read _____.

The word בָּנוּ is read _____.

The word לָנוּ is read _____.

10. Let's try a few more.

This syllable מֵנוּ is read _____.

This syllable שֶׁנוּ is read _____.

This syllable תֵּנוּ is read _____.

11. Here are three words. One of them reads AH-LAY-NOO. Which one? ( )

עָלֵינוּ	גָּדוֹל	גָּאַל
(c)	(b)	(a)

12. And here are three more words. Which one reads MAH-GAY-N? ( )

נוֹרָא	מָגֵן	נָתַן
(c)	(b)	(a)

Here's another review lesson. Be sure you can read all the exercises with ease before you go on to Lesson 10. It really gets hard later on. Don't forget to turn to the second page of this reading drill!

1 בַּ בוֹ בָּ בוּ בֵּ בוֹ בַּ בֹּ בוּ

2 גַּ גוֹ גָּ גוּ גֵּ גוֹ גַּ גֹּ גוּ

3 ג ב ב ג ב ג ב ג ג ג ב ג ב ב ב

4 בֵּ רַ וָ לוֹ תְּ אֵ יַ עוּ שוֹ מוּ

5 בוֹתֵ בוֹשֵׁ בוֹדֵ בוֹאֵ בוֹגֵ

6 גָּדוֹ גוֹמֵ גָּמָ תַּגֵּ גוֹאֵ אַגוֹ

7 שְׁבֵ גְּבוּ גְּמָ עֵבַ גְּדוּ מְבַ

8 בָּנוּ דֵנוּ יָנוּ מָנוּ עָלֵינוּ

Here are more words and their meanings.

1	בְּנֵי children of	גַּן garden	נֵר candle	גַּם also	גֵּר stranger	גּוֹי nation
2	לָנוּ to us	רַגְלֵינוּ our feet	דּוֹרֵנוּ our age our generation			אֲבוֹתֵינוּ our fathers
3	גָּר lives	לָגוּר to live	לְנַגֵּן to play (an instrument)	מְנַגֵּן plays (an instrument)		
4	גָּדוֹל great, big	גָּדַל grew, became big	גַּדְּלוּ magnify!	גָּאוֹן genius; *gaon* – a rabbinic title		
5	גּוֹאֵל redeemer	מָגֵן shield	גְּמָרָא part of the Talmud			
6	גָּמָל camel	תַּרְנְגֹל rooster	אֲגוֹרוֹת Israeli coins			
7	נוֹדֵד wanders	נָדַד wandered	נוֹשֵׂא carries	נָשָׂא carried		
8	נוֹתֵן gives	נָתַן gave	גּוֹמֵר finishes	גָּמַר finished		

LESSON 10

NEW VOWEL: ֶ EH as in PET

NEW LETTERS: ה H, ח CH

LETTERS YOU KNOW:

ל	מ	ת	תּ	שׂ	שׁ	ד	ר	ב	בּ
L	M	T	T	S	SH	D	R	V	B

ג	נ	עַ אַ	ן	וֹ	י	ם
G	N	SILENT	FINAL N	V	Y	FINAL M

VOWELS:

ְ	ֹ	וֹ	ַ	ָ	ֵ
SILENT	OO	O	AH	AH	AY

---

1. This vowel וֹ is _____. This vowel ַ is _____.

   This vowel ֹ is _____. This vowel ָ is _____.

   This vowel ְ is _____. This vowel ֵ is _____.

   The new vowel ֶ is _____ as in _____.

2. Practice reading these vowels.

   ְ ֶ ַ ָ ֶ ֵ ְ ֶ ַ ֹ ֵ וֹ ָ ַ ←

3. Here are the two new letters.

   This ח is CHET; its saying sound is _____.

   This ה is HAY; its saying sound is _____.

4. The Hebrew sound that does *not* appear in the English alphabet is called

   _____. It is written so: _____.

5. This syllable הֶ reads _____.

   This syllable חֶ reads _____.

6. Under each syllable write its sound.

חָ חָ חֶ חוּ חוֹ חֵ חַ ←

_____ _____ _____ _____ _____ _____ _____

7. Cover the English sounds you've just written and practice reading.
   a. Reading the CHET slows your speed a bit, doesn't it?
   b. Try the line again.

8. We'll add the RAYSH ר and the DAHLET ד to the new letters HAY ה and CHET ח.

   Complete each sound by filling in the correct vowel.

ה ר ח ה ד ח ←

_____ _____ _____ _____ _____ _____

HEH RAH CHO HAH DOO CHAY

9. Match these words with their correct sounds. Watch out these are tricky!

H-AY-M	( )	(1) חַם
CH-AY-N	( )	(2) חֵם
CH-AH-M	( )	(3) חֵן

10. The Hebrew word for room is חֶדֶר.

    חֶדֶר is read _____.

11. At the end of a word the HAY ה is not sounded. When you see the word for the special Sabbath and holiday bread חַלָּה you read it _____ and you don't sound the ה at the end.

12. One of these words reads HAH-YAH. הָיָה חָדָשׁ חַג ←

    This word reads HAH-YAH.

    _____

You'll recognize many words here that you've heard in song and in prayer. Now you can read them. And are you remembering all the numbers so far? Here are a few more.

1	ה	ה	ח	ה	ה	ח	ח	ח	ה	ח	ה	ה	
2	ב	ג	ג	ב	ב	ב	ג	ב	ג	ג	ב	ב	ב
3	א	ע	ע	א	ע	ע	א	א	א	ע	א	ע	
4	ו	ן	ו	ן	י	י	י	ן	ו	ן	ו	ו	ן	י	ו
5	וֹ	וּ	וּ	וּ	וּ	וֹ	וֹ	וּ	וּ	וֹ	וּ	וֹ	וֹ	וּ	וּ
6	ְ	ְ	ְ	ְ	ְ	ְ	ְ	ְ	ְ	ְ	ְ	ְ	ְ
7	:	־	ד	ְ	ְ	:	־:	ְ	ד:	ְְ	ְ	ְ
8	הוֹ	חוּ	הֵ	חַ	הֶ	חִ	הוּ	חֶ	חוֹ	חֵ
9	הָיָ	הַיוֹ	הַשָּׁ	חָדָ	חֹדֶ	חַמֵּ	חֶם
10	אֶל	עֶרֶ	אֶחַ	אַחַ	תַּחַ	חַבֵּ	חוֹשֶׁ

1	חָבֵר	חֲבֵרָה	יֶלֶד	יַלְדָּה	אַתְּ	אַתָּה
	friend (masc.)	friend (fem.)	boy	girl	you (fem.)	you (masc.)
2	אֱלֹהֵי	אֱלֹהֵינוּ	הַלְלוּ	הַלְלוּיָה		
	God of	our God	praise!	praise ye the Lord!		
3	אוֹהֵב	אוֹהֶבֶת	חוֹשֵׁב	חוֹשֶׁבֶת		
	likes (masc.)	likes (fem.)	thinks (masc.)	thinks (fem.)		
4	תּוֹרָה	הַיּוֹם	מָחָר	חַג	תּוֹדָה	
	Torah	today	tomorrow	holiday	thank you	
5	חֹדֶשׁ	חָדָשׁ	חֶדֶר	מַחְבֶּרֶת		
	month	new	room	notebook		
6	אֶתְרוֹג	הַלֵּילוֹת	הַגָּדָה			
	etrog	the nights	narrative			
7	אֶחָד	אַחַת	חָמֵשׁ	שֶׁבַע	הַשָּׁעָה	
	one (masc.)	one (fem.)	five	seven	the time	
8	עֶרֶב	רֶגֶל	גְּבֶרֶת	לֶחֶם	שֶׁמֶשׁ	
	evening	foot	Mrs.	bread	sun	
9	רוּחַ	שָׂמֵחַ	לוּחַ	שׁוֹלֵחַ	יָרֵחַ	
	spirit, wind	happy	blackboard	send	moon	

10 אֵין חָדָשׁ תַּחַת הַשֶּׁמֶשׁ.

There is nothing new under the sun.(Proverb)

LESSON 11

NEW LETTERS:

ך FINAL CHAHF כּ KAHF כ CHAHF

LETTERS YOU KNOW:

ם FINAL M ל L מ M ת T תּ T ש S שׂ SH ד D ר R ב V בּ B

ה H ח CH ג G נ N אע SILENT ן FINAL N ו V י Y

VOWELS:

ְ EH ְ SILENT וּ OO וֹ O ַ AH ָ AH ֵ AY

1. CHAHF כ and CHET ח have the same saying sound. This is the sound not found in the English alphabet.

   כ and ח have the saying sound of _____.

2. Add a dot to the CHAHF כ so: כּ and the letter becomes _____.

3. The saying sound of this letter כ is _____.

   The saying sound of this letter כּ is _____.

4. Here is a row of CHAHFs and KAHFs. Under each letter write its saying sound.

   כּ כ כ כ כּ כ כּ כּ כ ←

   _____ _____ _____ _____ _____ _____ _____ _____ _____

5. Let's practice reading כ and כּ combined with vowels you know.

   כּוכוּ כָּכָ כוּ כוֹ כָּ כָ כַ כָּ ←

6. Here are the BET בּ and VET ב. Do you confuse them with כּ and כ? Let's find out. Fill in the saying sounds.

   בּ ב כּ כּ כ ב כּ בּ

   _____ _____ _____ _____ _____ _____ _____ _____

7. Now try vowels combined with KAHF כּ CHAHF כ BET בּ and VET ב

   כּוֹ בוֹ כּוּ כַּ בָּ כָ בַ כָּ ←

   _____ _____ _____ _____ _____ _____ _____ _____

8. Can you read this word? כְּבוֹד We've added the DAHLET ד and a vowel to the כ and the ב .

Let's work it out— כְּ is _____

בוֹ is _____

ד is _____

The word כְּבוֹד is read _____. It means "glory of."

9. Let's try another חָכָם This syllable חָ reads _____

כָ reads _____

This Final Letter ם reads _____

The word חָכָם means "wise man," "sage." חָכָם reads _____.

If you are able to read חָכָם you are indeed wise.

10. Here are the FINAL letters you've learned so far: ם = Final _____

ן = Final _____

and this letter ך is Final CHAHF

11. Just as ם and ן appear only at the end of a word, so too ך FINAL _____.

12. Most times ך appears at the end of a word combined with the silent vowel ְ SHVAH, so: ְך The saying sound of this letter ְך is _____.

13. Here is the word BLESSED or PRAISED that you have used many times בָּרוּךְ.

The word בָּרוּךְ reads _____.

14. This is a Blessing you've repeated from memory for a long time. Now read it.

בָּרוּךְ שֵׁם כְּבוֹד מַלְכוּתוֹ לְעוֹלָם וָעֶד

Some of these sounds will be a little rough on your throat, but you'll get used to them. Onward!

1 כַּ כוֹ כֵּ כֶּ כוּ כָּ כוֹ כֶּ כֵּ כַּ כֵּ

2 כַ כוֹ כֵ כֶ כוּ כָ כוֹ כֶ כֵ כַ כֵ

3 ךְ ך ך ך ך ך ך ך ך ך ך ך

4 כ ח ה כּ כּ כ כּ ח כּ ה כ ח כּ

5 כ ב כּ ב כ ב כ ב כּ ב כ ב כּ

6 כְּבוֹ כְּמוֹ כָּחוֹ נָכוֹ כוּתוֹ

7 כּוֹבַ כּוֹתֵ כֹּתֶ כֹּהֵ בּוֹכֶ

8 מוּכָ מַלְכוּ אֶשְׁכּוֹ אוֹכֵ עַכְשָׁ

9 רוּךְ לֶךְ מֵךְ רָךְ לוֹךְ שֶׁךְ

10 הֶךְ בְּךָ לְךָ שְׁךָ דֶךָ לוּךָ

11 וְאָהַבְתָּ לְרֵעֲךָ כָּמוֹךָ

Love your neighbor as yourself.

1	מֶלֶךְ king	מַלְכֵּנוּ our king	מַלְכוּת kingdom	מַלְכוּתוֹ His kingdom
2	בָּרְכוּ bless!	בָּרוּךְ blessed	כְּבוֹד glory	כְּבוֹדוֹ His glory
3	כֹּל all	בְּכָל with all	וּבְכָל and with all	שֶׁבְּכָל that on all
4	כֵּן yes	כֹּהֵן *kohen,* priest	כַּוָּנָה intention	כֹּחַ strength	כָּחֹל blue
5	כֹּתֶל wall	כֶּתֶר crown	כָּשֵׁר kosher	דֶּרֶךְ road	בֶּרֶךְ knee
6	כּוֹתֵב he writes	כּוֹתֶבֶת she writes	אוֹכֵל he eats	אוֹכֶלֶת she eats
7	עַכְשָׁו now	כְּבָר already	כַּמָּה how many?	כְּמוֹ like, as
8	כּוֹבַע hat	כַּדּוּר ball	כֶּלֶב dog	אֶשְׁכּוֹל bunch of grapes	חֹשֶׁךְ darkness
9	חָכָם wise	נָכוֹן correct	יֵשׁ לְךָ you have (masc.)	יֵשׁ לָךְ you have (fem.)
10	מַה שְׁלוֹמְךָ? How are you? (masc.)	מַה שְׁלוֹמֵךְ? How are you? (fem.)
11	מַה שְׁמֵךְ? What's your name? (fem.)	

NEW VOWELS:

ִ	ֵ
IH	EE

LETTERS YOU KNOW:

ם	ל	מ	ת	ת	ש	שׂ	ד	ר	ב	בּ
FINAL M	L	M	T	T	S	SH	D	R	V	B

ך	כּ	כ	ה	ח	ג	נ	אע	ן	ו	י
FINAL CH	K	CH	H	CH	G	N	SILENT	FINAL N	V	Y

VOWELS:

ֶ	ְ	ֻ	ֹ	ַ	ָ	ֲ
EH	SILENT	OO	O	AH	AH	AY

Let's stop for another quiz to catch up on all you've learned so far.

1. Here are two rows of look-alike letters. First look at the letter in Row A. Then add a dot to each letter in Row B and write its name in the space provided.

ROW B		ROW A
_____ ב	VET	ב
_____ כ	CHAHF	כ
_____ ת	TAHV	ת

2. These are letters often confused for one another. You fill in the missing names.

_____ ד	RAYSH	ר
_____ נ	GIMEL	ג
_____ ה	CHET	ח
_____ ר	VAHV	ו

3. Here are pairs of letters with the same saying sound. Write the correct saying sounds.

a. _____ ח כ

b. _____ א ע

c. _____ תּ ת

d. _____ ב ו

4. Each of these is a FINAL letter. Fill in the saying sounds.

ן ך ם

_____ _____ _____

5. Here again are the FINAL letters. Each one has a regular letter with the same name. Next to each FINAL letter, write the regular letter.

REGULAR		FINAL
_____	MEM	ם
_____	CHAHF	ך
_____	NUN	ן

6. We'll give you the vowel *sounds*. You fill in the vowels.

AH (2) _____ OO _____

O _____ IH _____

AY _____ EH _____

SILENT _____

7. You know that one dot • is the vowel IH as in TICK. How do you read one dot followed by the YUD so: ִי • ִי • is read _____.

8. Here are letters you know. Some are combined with the vowel ◌ others with the vowel ◌ִי . Under each, write its sound.

מִ מִי לִ לִי כִּ כִּי

_____ _____ _____ _____ _____ _____

9. The YUD י is used in other ways.

When י follows ◌ַ the sound is AH EE (I) ◌ַי

When י follows ◌ָ the sound is AH EE (I) ◌ָי

This word אֲדוֹנָי reads _____.

This word שַׁדַּי reads _____.

10. This is one way to write the name by which God is known יְיָ .

Here is another אֲדוֹנָי . Both אֲדוֹנָי and יְיָ mean _____.

Though אֲדוֹנָי and יְיָ are written differently, they are always read as _____ . This too אֲדֹנָי is read as _____.

11. Have you remembered that sometimes the י is read as Y?

Under each syllable fill in its sound, and don't let the י trick you.

יַ יוֹ כִּי יְ הִי תִי יִ

_____ _____ _____ _____ _____ _____ _____

12. This is the Hebrew word for Israel יִשְׂרָאֵל .

The word יִשְׂרָאֵל is read _____ .

13. Here's a prayer you've known by heart for a long time. It was probably the first one you memorized. Now you can read it.

שְׁמַע יִשְׂרָאֵל יְיָ אֱלֹהֵינוּ יְיָ אֶחָד

Here are the numbers 1 through 12 to help you tell time.

1	אַחַת	שְׁתַּיִם	שָׁלֹשׁ	אַרְבַּע
	(1)	(2)	(3)	(4)
2	חָמֵשׁ	שֵׁשׁ	שֶׁבַע	שְׁמֹנֶה
	(5)	(6)	(7)	(8)
3	תֵּשַׁע	עֶשֶׂר	אַחַת עֶשְׂרֵה	רֶבַע
	(9)	(10)	(11)	a fourth a quarter
4	שְׁתֵּים עֶשְׂרֵה	שָׁעָה	וְ	מַה הַשָּׁעָה?
	(12)	time, hour	and	What time is it?

Using the masculine verb יָכוֹל and the feminine יְכוֹלָה (can, able) with the following infinitives, endless sentences can be formed.

5	לִלְמֹד	לִשְׁמֹעַ	לִשְׁלֹחַ	לָשִׁיר
	to study	to hear	to send	to sing
6	לְחַכּוֹת	לִרְאוֹת	לִכְתֹּב	לְהַכִּיר
	to wait	to see	to write	to know to be acquainted
7	לְדַבֵּר	לַעֲשׂוֹת	לָלֶכֶת	לְהַתְחִיל
	to speak	to do	to go, to walk	to begin
8	עִבְרִית	אַנְגְלִית	אֲנִי	בַּיִת	הַבַּיְתָה
	Hebrew	English	I	house	homeward
9	אֲנִי יָכוֹל לִכְתֹּב וּלְדַבֵּר עִבְרִית.				

I can write and speak Hebrew.

THE SH'MA BLESSING

1 שְׁמַע יִשְׂרָאֵל יְיָ אֱלֹהֵינוּ יְיָ אֶחָד.

Hear, O Israel:
The Lord is our God, the Lord is One.

A RESPONSE AND A BLESSING

2 בָּרוּךְ שֵׁם כְּבוֹד מַלְכוּתוֹ לְעוֹלָם וָעֶד.

Blessed be His name whose glorious
kingdom is forever and ever.

BLESSINGS BEFORE READING THE TORAH

3 בָּרְכוּ אֶת יְיָ הַמְבֹרָךְ.

Bless the Lord, who is blessed!

4 בָּרוּךְ יְיָ הַמְבֹרָךְ לְעוֹלָם וָעֶד.

Blessed be the Lord who is blessed
for ever and ever.

5 בָּרוּךְ אַתָּה יְיָ

Blessed are You, Lord,

6 אֱלֹהֵינוּ מֶלֶךְ הָעוֹלָם

our God, King of the universe,

7 אֲשֶׁר בָּחַר בָּנוּ

who chose us

8 מִכָּל הָעַמִּים

from all the peoples,

9 וְנָתַן לָנוּ אֶת תּוֹרָתוֹ

and gave us His Torah.

10 בָּרוּךְ אַתָּה יְיָ נוֹתֵן הַתּוֹרָה.

Blessed are You, Lord, who gives the Torah.

Now you can read the שְׁמַע, sing אֵין כֵּאלֹהֵינוּ, and count from 1 through 12. Good for you!

אֱלֹהֵי	אֲדוֹנָי	מֶלֶךְ	מוֹשִׁיעַ
God of	Lord	king	savior

אֱלֹהֵינוּ	אֲדוֹנֵינוּ	מַלְכֵּנוּ	מוֹשִׁיעֵנוּ
our God	our Lord	our King	our Savior

אֵין	מִי	נוֹדֶה	בָּרוּךְ	אַתָּה הוּא
none	who	we will give thanks	blessed	You are He

1	אֵין כֵּאלֹהֵינוּ	אֵין כַּאדוֹנֵינוּ
2	אֵין כְּמַלְכֵּנוּ	אֵין כְּמוֹשִׁיעֵנוּ
3	מִי כֵאלֹהֵינוּ	מִי כַאדוֹנֵינוּ
4	מִי כְמַלְכֵּנוּ	מִי כְמוֹשִׁיעֵנוּ
5	נוֹדֶה לֵאלֹהֵינוּ	נוֹדֶה לַאדוֹנֵינוּ
6	נוֹדֶה לְמַלְכֵּנוּ	נוֹדֶה לְמוֹשִׁיעֵנוּ
7	בָּרוּךְ אֱלֹהֵינוּ	בָּרוּךְ אֲדוֹנֵינוּ
8	בָּרוּךְ מַלְכֵּנוּ	בָּרוּךְ מוֹשִׁיעֵנוּ
9	אַתָּה הוּא אֱלֹהֵינוּ	אַתָּה הוּא אֲדוֹנֵינוּ
10	אַתָּה הוּא מַלְכֵּנוּ	אַתָּה הוּא מוֹשִׁיעֵנוּ

LESSON 13

NEW VOWEL: U as in PUT

NEW LETTERS: פּ P, פ F

LETTERS YOU KNOW:

ם	מ	ל	ת	תּ	ש	שׂ	ד	ר	ב	בּ	
FINAL M	L	M	T	T	S	SH	D	R	V	B	

ך	כּ	כ	ה	ח	ג	נ	אע		ן	ו	י
FINAL CH	K	CH	H	CH	G	N	SILENT		FINAL N	V	Y

VOWELS:

ִי	ִ	ֵ	ְ	וּ	וֹ	ָ	ַ	ֶ
EE	IH	EH	SILENT	OO	O	AH	AH	AY

---

1. FAY is written פ. It has *no* dot in the middle. Its saying sound is_____.

2. Match these columns

F ( )	(1)	פֶ
FAY ( )	(2)	פוֹ
FO ( )	(3)	פְ

3. Here is a row of FAYs. Each פ is combined with a vowel you know. Write the complete sounds under each syllable.

פִי פֵ פָ פְ פוּ פִ פַ

_____ _____ _____ _____ _____ _____ _____

4. PAY is written פּ. It has a dot in the middle. Its saying sound is_____.

5. Under each letter write its saying sound.

פ פ פ פּ פ פּ פ פּ

_____ _____ _____ _____ _____ _____ _____ _____

6. Read aloud these sounds, combining vowels you know with the פ and פּ.

פָ פוֹ פָ פַ פוּ פֵ פֶ פִ

Now try reading the line a little faster.

7. We'll add more letters to this row. Fill in the sounds under each one, and remember what you learned about ִ. EE.

בַּ כָּ פָּ פִּי בוּ כָּ רִי

_____ _____ _____ _____ _____ _____ _____

8. Here's a word you've heard many times. פָּרִי

Let's sound it out פָּ is _____

רִי is _____

The word פָּרִי is read _____

9. Can you read this word חֲמֵשׁ It means "Five Books of Moses."

Work it out here: חֲ is read _____

מֵ is read _____

שׁ is read _____

The word חֲמֵשׁ is read _____.

10. The vowel IH ִ has _____ dot;

AY ֵ has _____ dots;

The new vowel U ֶ has _____ dots.

11. Now you know two vowels consisting of three dots.

This vowel ֶ is _____ as in _____.

This vowel ֵ is _____ as in _____.

12. You also know two vowels consisting of two dots.

This vowel ֵ is _____ as in _____.

This vowel ְ is called _____ and it is _____.

13. Here are ALL the vowels you have learned. Under each write its sound.

ִ וּ וֹ ְ ֵ ֶ ַ ָ ֻ

_____ _____ _____ _____ _____ _____ _____ _____ _____ _____

By this time you should be able to write very simple sentences with all the words you've learned. Have you tried it?

1 פ פ פ פ פ פ פ פ פ פ פ פ פ פ

2 ׳ ־ ״ ׃ ׳ ד ׃ ׳ ־ ״ ׃ ׳ ד ׃ ׳

3	שׁוֹפָר shofar	פְּרִי fruit	פֹּה here	עִפָּרוֹן pencil
4	פּוּרִים Purim	חֲנֻכָּה Chanukah	חֻמָּשׁ the Five Books of Moses	פָּרָשָׁה chapter, portion
5	יָפֶה nice (masc.)	יָפָה nice (fem.)	רוֹפֵא doctor	חָפְשִׁי free
6	אֵיפֹה where is?	אֶפְשָׁר maybe	אֲפִילוּ even	לִפְעָמִים sometimes
7	כִּפָּה skull cap	פֶּה mouth	פָּנִים face	אֲרֻחָה meal
8	מִשְׁפָּחָה family	תְּפִלָּה prayer	פּוֹתֵחַ opens	לַיְלָה night

BLESSING OVER WINE

9 בָּרוּךְ אַתָּה יְיָ אֱלֹהֵינוּ מֶלֶךְ הָעוֹלָם

Blessed are You, Lord, our God, King of the universe

10 בּוֹרֵא פְּרִי הַגָּפֶן.

who creates the fruit of the vine.

LESSON 14

NEW LETTERS:

ק	ט
K	T

LETTERS YOU KNOW:

ל	מ	ת	תּ	שׂ	שׁ	ד	ר	ב	בּ
L	M	T	T	S	SH	D	R	V	B

ג	נ	אע	ן	ו	י	ם
G	N	SILENT	FINAL N	V	Y	FINAL M

פּ	פ	ך	כּ	כ	ה	ח
P	F	FINAL CH	K	CH	H	CH

VOWELS:

ֻ	ֶ	ִ	ֵ	ְ	וּ	וֹ	ָ	ַ	ֲ
U	EE	IH	EH	SILENT	OO	O	AH	AH	AY

---

1. Here is the letter ט TET, sometimes confused with the MEM מ.

   The saying sound of ט is_____.

   The saying sound of מ is_____.

2. Do you mistake ט for מ? Let's find out. Under each letter fill in its saying sound.

   מ ט מ ט ט ט מ ט

   _____ _____ _____ _____ _____ _____ _____ _____

3. We've combined MEM מ and TET ט with vowels. Write their sounds under each.

   טָ טִי טוֹ מַ טִ טָ

   _____ _____ _____ _____ _____ _____

4. Read over the sounds you've just written above. Sure they're correct? Cover them now and practice reading the Hebrew syllables. Is your speed improving?

5. To complete each syllable in this row, you supply the correct vowel.

MEH	TAH	MU	TOO	MIH	TAY	MO	TAH	MAH
מ	ט	מ	ט	מ	ט	מ	תּ	מ
_____	_____	_____	_____	_____	_____	_____	_____	_____

6. Try speed-reading the row you've just finished. Cover the English sounds.

7. Here are the LAHMED ל, the TAHV ת, and the VET ב.

We'll combine them with ט and מ for practice reading. Ready?

טַלִּי תָּבָ מָבוֹ לַמַ טַת לֶבָב

8. The Hebrew word for "good" is טוֹב. Were you able to read טוֹב?

The word טוֹב reads _____

9. Here's another Hebrew word טַלִּית. It means prayer shawl. Let's work it out.

טַ reads _____

לִי reads _____

ת reads _____

The word טַלִּית reads _____.

10. This is the KOOF ק. This is the KAHF כ.

Both have the saying sound of _____.

11. The Blessing recited over wine begins the KIH-DOO-SH. To complete the word KIH-DOO-SH, you fill in the vowels.

קדוש

12. These are the last two words of the first Blessing in the קִדּוּשׁ

פְּרִי הַגָּפֶן

They read _____ _____.

13. Can you read the entire Blessing?

בָּרוּךְ אַתָּה יְיָ אֱלֹהֵינוּ מֶלֶךְ הָעוֹלָם

בּוֹרֵא פְּרִי הַגָּפֶן.

How often have you heard your teacher say **טוֹב מְאֹד**?
Now you can read it. Very good!

1 טַ טֶ טוֹ טוּ טֵ טָ טֶ קוֹ קַ קֶ קֹ קִ

2 ט ט מ ט מ ט ט ט מ ט מ ט

3 ק כּ כ ק ק כ כּ כ ק כּ ק ק

4 טוֹב — good
בֹּקֶר טוֹב — good morning
עֶרֶב טוֹב — good evening
לַיְלָה טוֹב — good night

5 יוֹם טוֹב — holiday
שְׁבָט — Hebrew month
טוּ בִּשְׁבָט — 15th of Shevat
טֵבֵת — Hebrew month

6 קָדוֹשׁ — holy
קִדּוּשׁ — sanctification
קֹדֶשׁ — holiness
קִדְּשָׁנוּ — sanctified us
מְקַדֵּשׁ — sanctifies

7 טַלִּית — prayer shawl
לְהַדְלִיק — to kindle
קוֹרֵא — reads (masc.)
קוֹרֵאת — reads (fem.)

8 בְּבַקָּשָׁה — please
יְרָקוֹת — vegetables
אֲפִיקוֹמָן — Afikomen, piece of mahtsah eaten after Seder meal
לִקְרֹא — to read

9 הַקָּפוֹת — processions
קָפֶה — coffee
מִשְׁפָּט — judgment
נְקֻדּוֹת — vowels
קַל — easy

10 קָטָן — little (masc.)
קְטַנָּה — little (fem.)
קֶרֶן — fund, horn
נָטַע — planted (masc.)
יַעֲקֹב — Jacob

BLESSINGS AFTER READING THE TORAH

1 בָּרוּךְ אַתָּה יְיָ Blessed are You, Lord,

2 אֱלֹהֵינוּ מֶלֶךְ הָעוֹלָם our God, King of the universe,

3 אֲשֶׁר נָתַן לָנוּ תּוֹרַת אֱמֶת who has given us the Torah of truth

4 וְחַיֵּי עוֹלָם נָטַע בְּתוֹכֵנוּ. and has implanted within us eternal life.

5 בָּרוּךְ אַתָּה יְיָ Blessed are You, Lord,

6 נוֹתֵן הַתּוֹרָה. who gives the Torah.

SONGS BASED ON BIBLICAL VERSES

7 הִנֵּה מַה טּוֹב וּמַה נָּעִים Behold how good and how pleasant it is
שֶׁבֶת אַחִים גַּם יָחַד for brothers to dwell together as one.
(Psalm 133)

8 לֹא יִשָּׂא גוֹי אֶל גוֹי חֶרֶב Nation shall not lift up sword against nation.
לֹא יִלְמְדוּ עוֹד מִלְחָמָה They shall not learn war anymore.
(Isaiah 2:4; Micah 4:3)

9 מַה טֹּבוּ אֹהָלֶיךָ יַעֲקֹב How goodly are your tents, Jacob,
מִשְׁכְּנֹתֶיךָ יִשְׂרָאֵל Your tabernacles, Israel.
(Numbers 24:5)

LESSON 15

NEW LETTERS:

ז	ץ	צ
Z	FINAL TS	TS

LETTERS YOU KNOW:

ל	מ	ת	ת	שׂ	שׁ	ד	ר	ב	בּ
L	M	T	T	S	SH	D	R	V	B

ג	נ	אע	ן	ו	י	ם
G	N	SILENT	FINAL N	V	Y	FINAL M

ט	ק	פּ	פ	ך	כּ	כ	ה	ח
T	K	P	F	FINAL CH	K	CH	H	CH

VOWELS:

◌ּ◌ּ	◌ֵ	◌ִ	◌ֶ	◌ְ	◌ֹ	◌ֹ	◌ַ	◌ָ	◌ֲ
U	EE	IH	EH	SILENT	OO	O	AH	AH	AY

---

1. Here's the new letter with the unusual sound צ . It is called TSAHDEE.

   Its saying sound is _____ as in _____.

2. The TSAHDEE צ is the Hebrew letter found in the word MATSOT. Put a circle around the TSAHDEE in the Hebrew word מַצּוֹת

3. The צ is found too, in the word MITSVAH מִצְוָה

   The name of this letter צ is _____ and its saying sound is _____.

4. Do you recognize this well-known phrase? בַּר מִצְוָה

   The phrase בַּר מִצְוָה reads _____ _____.

5. How about this phrase, recognize it? בַּת מִצְוָה

   The phrase בַּת מִצְוָה reads _____ _____.

6. Sometimes the TSAHDEE צ is mistaken for the silent letter AHYIN: ע
Do you make that mistake? Under each letter in this row write its saying sound.

ע צ ע צ ע צ צ

_____ _____ _____ _____ _____ _____ _____

7. Add the correct vowels to complete these syllables.

AY	TSU	TSEE	AH	OO	TSO	TSAY	TSAH
ע	צ	צי	ע	ע	צ	צ	צ
_____	_____	_____	_____	_____	_____	_____	_____

8. Now practice speed-reading the line above. Remember accuracy is most important.

9. The Blessing recited over bread is called הַמּוֹצִיא.

Can you read הַמּוֹצִיא? Let's work it out.

הַ reads _____

מוֹ reads _____

צִיא reads _____

The word הַמּוֹצִיא reads _____

10. Here is the FINAL TSAHDEE ץ. It appears only at the _____ of a word.

11. Can you read this word? It means land. אֶרֶץ

The word אֶרֶץ reads _____.

LAND OF ISRAEL is written: אֶרֶץ יִשְׂרָאֵל

It reads _____ _____

12. Sometimes the ZAHYIN ז is mistaken for the VAHV ו Be on your guard.
Under each of these syllables write their sounds.

זַ זַ זֶ זוֹ זִ זֵ זָ

_____ _____ _____ _____ _____ _____ _____

Here are some letters that are easily confused. Are you sure you can read each one correctly? Don't be fooled.

1 ז ז צ צ ץ ץ צ ז ז צ ץ ץ

2 צ ע צ צ צ ע צ ע ע צ ע ע

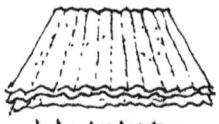

3 אֶרֶץ — land; צִיּוֹן — Zion; אַרְצוֹת הַבְּרִית — United States; מִצָּה זוּ

4 מַזָּל — luck; מָזוֹן — food; מְצֻיָּן — excellent; מַצָּה — (plural) unleavened bread (sing.); מַצּוֹת

5 מִצְוָה — commandment; מִצְוֹת — commandments; מִצְוֹתָיו — His commandments; בְּמִצְוֹתָיו — by His commandments

6 זֶה — this (masc.); זֹאת — this (fem.); זְמַן — time, season; בַּזְּמַן הַזֶּה — at this time

7 זְמִירוֹת — hymns, songs; מְזוּזָה — mezuzah; זָהָב — gold; בֵּיצָה — egg; זֵכֶר — in remembrance

8 זִכָּרוֹן — memorial, reminder; רוֹצֶה — want, wish (masc.); רוֹצָה — want, wish (fem.); צוֹחֵק — laughs (masc.); יִצְחָק — Isaac

9 עֵץ — tree; עֵצִים — trees; זוּזִים — silver coins; יוֹם הָעַצְמָאוּת — Independence Day

10 צוּר — rock, God; הַמּוֹצִיא — who brings forth; הוֹצִיאָנוּ — brought us out; מִמִּצְרָיִם — from Egypt

BLESSING OVER SABBATH LIGHTS

1	בָּרוּךְ אַתָּה יְיָ	Blessed are You, Lord,
2	אֱלֹהֵינוּ מֶלֶךְ הָעוֹלָם	our God, King of the universe
3	אֲשֶׁר קִדְּשָׁנוּ	who has sanctified us
4	בְּמִצְוֹתָיו	by His commandments
5	וְצִוָּנוּ	and commanded us
6	לְהַדְלִיק	to kindle
7	נֵר שֶׁל שַׁבָּת.	the Sabbath light.

BLESSING OVER WINE

1	בָּרוּךְ אַתָּה יְהוָה	Blessed are You, Lord,
2	אֱלֹהֵינוּ מֶלֶךְ הָעוֹלָם	our God, King of the universe,
3	בּוֹרֵא פְּרִי הַגָּפֶן.	who creates the fruit of the vine.

BLESSING OVER BREAD

1	בָּרוּךְ אַתָּה יְהוָה	Blessed are You, Lord,
2	אֱלֹהֵינוּ מֶלֶךְ הָעוֹלָם	our God, King of the universe
3	הַמּוֹצִיא לֶחֶם מִן הָאָרֶץ.	who brings forth bread from the earth.

BLESSING ON SPECIAL OCCASIONS

1	בָּרוּךְ אַתָּה יְיָ	Blessed are You, Lord,
2	אֱלֹהֵינוּ מֶלֶךְ הָעוֹלָם	our God, King of the universe
3	שֶׁהֶחֱיָנוּ	who has given us life
4	וְקִיְּמָנוּ	and sustained us
5	וְהִגִּיעָנוּ	and brought us
6	לַזְּמַן הַזֶּה.	to this season.

1 בָּרוּךְ אַתָּה יְיָ׃ Blessed are You, Lord,

2 אֱלֹהֵינוּ מֶלֶךְ הָעוֹלָם our God, King of the universe

3 אֲשֶׁר קִדְּשָׁנוּ בְּמִצְוֹתָיו who made us holy by His commandments

4 וְרָצָה בָנוּ and favored us

5 וְשַׁבַּת קָדְשׁוֹ בְּאַהֲבָה וּבְרָצוֹן הִנְחִילָנוּ and gave us as an inheritance His holy Sabbath in love and in favor,

6 זִכָּרוֹן לְמַעֲשֵׂה בְרֵאשִׁית. a reminder of the works of Creation.

7 כִּי הוּא יוֹם תְּחִלָּה לְמִקְרָאֵי קֹדֶשׁ For it is a first day among the festivals of holiness,

8 זֵכֶר לִיצִיאַת מִצְרָיִם. a reminder of the Exodus from Egypt.

9 כִּי בָנוּ בָחַרְתָּ For You have chosen us

10 וְאוֹתָנוּ קִדַּשְׁתָּ מִכָּל הָעַמִּים and have made us holy among all the peoples,

11 וְשַׁבַּת קָדְשְׁךָ בְּאַהֲבָה וּבְרָצוֹן הִנְחַלְתָּנוּ. and have given us as an inheritance Your holy Sabbath in love and in favor.

12 בָּרוּךְ אַתָּה יְיָ׃ Blessed are You, Lord,

13 מְקַדֵּשׁ הַשַּׁבָּת. who makes the Sabbath holy.

14 בָּרוּךְ אַתָּה יְיָ׃ Blessed are you, Lord,

15 אֱלֹהֵינוּ מֶלֶךְ הָעוֹלָם our God, King of the universe

16 בּוֹרֵא פְּרִי הַגָּפֶן. who creates the fruit of the vine.

Blessed are You, Lord, our God, King of the universe	בָּרוּךְ אַתָּה יְיָ אֱלֹהֵינוּ מֶלֶךְ הָעוֹלָם	1
who has chosen good prophets	אֲשֶׁר בָּחַר בִּנְבִיאִים טוֹבִים	2
and has found delight in their words spoken in truth.	וְרָצָה בְדִבְרֵיהֶם הַנֶּאֱמָרִים בֶּאֱמֶת.	3
Blessed are You, Lord, who has chosen the Torah	בָּרוּךְ אַתָּה יְיָ הַבּוֹחֵר בַּתּוֹרָה	4
and Moses Your servant and Israel Your people	וּבְמֹשֶׁה עַבְדּוֹ וּבְיִשְׂרָאֵל עַמּוֹ	5
and Your prophets of truth and righteousness.	וּבִנְבִיאֵי הָאֱמֶת וָצֶדֶק.	6

LESSON 16

NEW LETTERS:

ס	ך
S	FINAL F

LETTERS YOU KNOW:

ב	ב	ר	ד	ש	שׂ	ת	ת	מ	ל	ם
B	V	R	D	SH	S	T	T	M	L	FINAL M

י	ו	ן	אע	נ	ג	ח	ה
Y	V	FINAL N	SILENT	N	G	CH	H

כ	כּ	ך	פּפ	ק	ט	צ	ץ	ז
CH	K	FINAL CH	F	P	K	T	TS	FINAL TS	Z

VOWELS:

ּ	ֶ	ִ	ֵ	ְ	ֹ	ָ	ַ	ָ	ֲ
U	EE	IH	EH	SILENT	OO	O	AH	AH	AY

---

1. We'll begin this lesson by reviewing the Hebrew letters in the order in which they appear in the Hebrew alphabet.
   You fill in the letter called for, under these first *seven* names.

   ZAHYIN VAHV HAY DAHLET GIMEL BET AHLEF

   _____ _____ _____ _____ _____ _____ _____

2. Check with the letters at the top of the page to be certain you've written the letters correctly.

   Now cover the names and read aloud the names of the letters you've written.

   Try it again checking your answer with the name over each letter.

   Now without looking call out the letters beginning with AHLEF and ending with ZAHYIN.

   Did you get them all? GOOD!

3. Here are the next *seven* letters. Again write the Hebrew letter under each name.

NUN MEM LAHMED KAHF YUD TET CHET

_____ _____ _____ _____ _____ _____ _____

4. Once again check with the letters at the top of the page.

Review these letters now in the same way that you did with the first seven.

Can you do it without looking, beginning with CHET and ending with NUN?

Now try the 14 letters, beginning with AHLEF and ending with NUN.

5. The remaining *eight* letters beginning with the new letter SAHMECH complete the Hebrew alphabet.

TAHV SHEEN RAYSH KOOF TSAHDEE PAY AHYIN SAHMECH

_____ _____ _____ _____ _____ _____ _____ _____

6. Do once again what you did with the first 14 letters.

Memorize all 22 letters. Know them by heart!

Ready to test yourself? Take a final look at all the letters.

Now in its proper order beginning with א and ending with ת write each letter.

_____ _____ _____ _____ _____ _____ _____ _____ _____
(9) (8) (7) (6) (5) (4) (3) (2) (1)

_____ _____ _____ _____ _____ _____ _____ _____ _____
(18) (17) (16) (15) (14) (13) (12) (11) (10)

_____ _____ _____ _____
(22) (21) (20) (19)

7. This time, in the same order, write the saying sounds for each of the 22 letters.

_____ _____ _____ _____ _____ _____ _____ _____ _____
(9) (8) (7) (6) (5) (4) (3) (2) (1)

_____ _____ _____ _____ _____ _____ _____ _____ _____
(18) (17) (16) (15) (14) (13) (12) (11) (10)

_____ _____ _____ _____
(22) (21) (20) (19)

8. You noticed that only 22 letters were included in the Hebrew alphabet. Let's discover why. In each of these pairs of letters below the DOT changes the saying sound, but the outlines of both letters are the same, therefore only *one* is used in the alphabet.

Fill in the name of the letter not used in the alphabet; we'll write the other.

_____	ב	BET	בּ
_____	כ	KAHF	כּ
_____	פ	PAY	פּ
_____	שׂ	SHEEN	שׁ

9. Here now is a review of the FINAL LETTERS including the FINAL FAY. Next to each FINAL LETTER write its saying sound.

FINAL _____ ך FINAL _____ ן FINAL _____ ם ←

FINAL _____ ץ FINAL _____ ף

10. Here are the regular letters of the FINAL LETTERS we've just reviewed. Fill in their saying sounds.

_____ נ _____ צ _____ מ _____ כ ←

_____ פ

11. Now write the regular Hebrew letters next to their FINAL outlines.

_____ ץ _____ ן _____ ם _____ ך _____ ף ←

12. How well have you learned the vowels? Let's find out. Here are all the sounds. You fill in the vowels.

_____	_____	_____	_____	_____	_____	_____	_____	_____	_____
SILENT	OO	EE	IH	AY	U	O	EH	AH	AH

←

13. In our tradition the SHEH-HEH-CHEH-YAH-NOO is the prayer recited on the occasion of a happy experience. That you have learned to read Hebrew is such an occasion. This is a difficult prayer to read, do it slowly, but remember it well.

בָּרוּךְ אַתָּה יְיָ אֱלֹהֵינוּ מֶלֶךְ הָעוֹלָם

שֶׁהֶחֱיָנוּ וְקִיְּמָנוּ וְהִגִּיעָנוּ לַזְּמַן הַזֶּה .

You've reached the end, and if you can read ALL of the words, on ALL of the Drill Sheets, you should be mighty proud of yourself.

א	ב	ג	ד	ה	ו	ז	ח	ט	י	כ	ל	מ	נ	ס
1	2	3	4	5	6	7	8	9	10	20	30	40	50	60

ע	פ	צ	ק	ר	ש	ת
70	80	90	100	200	300	400

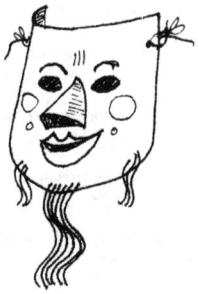

1	סִדּוּר	סֵדֶר	סִדְרָה	לְסַדֵּר	פֶּסַח
	prayerbook	Seder	weekly portion	to arrange	Passover
2	סֵפֶר	בֵּית סֵפֶר	סִפְרִיָּה	סִפּוּר	
	book	school	library	story	
3	נֵס	נִסִּים	נוֹסֵעַ	סִינַי	לְסַפֵּר
	miracle	miracles	travel	Sinai	to tell
4	סֻכָּה	סֻכּוֹת	סְפַרְדִּי	כְּנֶסֶת	
	Sukkah, booth	Feast of Booths	Spanish	Israeli Parliament	
5	כִּסֵּא	מַסֵּכָה	אֶסְתֵּר	סְבִיבוֹן	
	chair	mask	Esther	dreidel	
6	סִיּוּם	סְלִיחָה	סְלִיחוֹת	סוֹד	
	completion	Excuse me!	penitential prayers	secret	
7	דַּף	כַּף	אַף	גּוּף	יוֹסֵף	סוֹף
	page	spoon	nose	body	Joseph	end
8	מַזָּל טוֹב					
	Congratulations!					

READING THAT FOLLOWS THE SH'MA BLESSING

1	וְאָהַבְתָּ אֵת יְהוָה אֱלֹהֶיךָ	You shall love the Lord, your God,
2	בְּכָל לְבָבְךָ	with all your heart
3	וּבְכָל נַפְשְׁךָ	with all your soul,
4	וּבְכָל מְאֹדֶךָ	and with all your might.
5	וְהָיוּ הַדְּבָרִים הָאֵלֶּה	And these words
6	אֲשֶׁר אָנֹכִי מְצַוְּךָ הַיּוֹם	which I command you this day
7	עַל לְבָבֶךָ.	shall be upon your heart.
8	וְשִׁנַּנְתָּם לְבָנֶיךָ	You shall teach them diligently to your children,
9	וְדִבַּרְתָּ בָּם	and shall speak of them
10	בְּשִׁבְתְּךָ בְּבֵיתֶךָ	when you sit in your house,
11	וּבְלֶכְתְּךָ בַדֶּרֶךְ	when you walk by the way,
12	וּבְשָׁכְבְּךָ	when you lie down,
13	וּבְקוּמֶךָ.	and when you rise up.
14	וּקְשַׁרְתָּם לְאוֹת עַל יָדֶךָ	You shall bind them for a sign upon your hand
15	וְהָיוּ לְטֹטָפֹת בֵּין עֵינֶיךָ.	and they shall be for frontlets between your eyes.
16	וּכְתַבְתָּם עַל מְזֻזוֹת בֵּיתֶךָ	You shall write them upon the doorposts of your house
17	וּבִשְׁעָרֶיךָ.	and upon your gates.
18	לְמַעַן תִּזְכְּרוּ	That you may remember
19	וַעֲשִׂיתֶם אֶת כָּל מִצְוֹתָי	and do all My commandments
20	וִהְיִיתֶם קְדֹשִׁים לֵאלֹהֵיכֶם.	and be holy unto your God.
21	אֲנִי יְהוָה אֱלֹהֵיכֶם.	I am the Lord your God.

THE FOUR QUESTIONS

1 מַה נִּשְׁתַּנָּה הַלַּיְלָה הַזֶּה Why is this night different

2 מִכָּל הַלֵּילוֹת? from all other nights?

3 שֶׁבְּכָל הַלֵּילוֹת אָנוּ אוֹכְלִין For on all other nights we eat

4 חָמֵץ וּמַצָּה either leavened or unleavened bread (mahtsah);

5 הַלַּיְלָה הַזֶּה כֻּלּוֹ מַצָּה. on this night (we eat) only unleavened bread.

6 שֶׁבְּכָל הַלֵּילוֹת אָנוּ אוֹכְלִין For on all other nights we eat

7 שְׁאָר יְרָקוֹת all kinds of herbs (green vegetables);

8 הַלַּיְלָה הַזֶּה מָרוֹר. on this night (we eat) bitter herbs (horse-radish).

9 שֶׁבְּכָל הַלֵּילוֹת אֵין אָנוּ מַטְבִּילִין For on all other nights we do not dip

10 אֲפִילוּ פַּעַם אֶחָת even one time;

11 הַלַּיְלָה הַזֶּה שְׁתֵּי פְּעָמִים. on this night (we dip) two times.

12 שֶׁבְּכָל הַלֵּילוֹת אָנוּ אוֹכְלִין For on all other nights we eat

13 בֵּין יוֹשְׁבִין וּבֵין מְסֻבִּין either sitting up or reclining (leaning);

14 הַלַּיְלָה הַזֶּה כֻּלָּנוּ מְסֻבִּין. on this night we all recline.

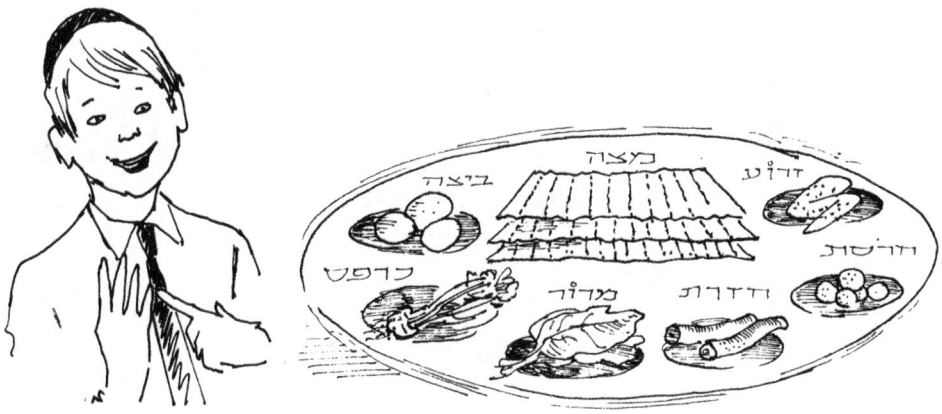

1 כָּל עוֹד בַּלֵּבָב פְּנִימָה — So long as within his heart

2 נֶפֶשׁ יְהוּדִי הוֹמִיָּה, — The soul of the Jew longs,

3 וּלְפַאֲתֵי מִזְרָח קָדִימָה — And he turns eastward,

4 עַיִן לְצִיּוֹן צוֹפִיָּה; — His eye looking toward Zion,

5 עוֹד לֹא אָבְדָה תִקְוָתֵנוּ, — Our hope is not yet lost.

6 הַתִּקְוָה שְׁנוֹת אַלְפַּיִם, — The hope of two thousand years –

7 לִהְיוֹת עַם חָפְשִׁי בְּאַרְצֵנוּ, — To be a free people in our land,

8 אֶרֶץ צִיּוֹן וִירוּשָׁלָיִם. — The land of Zion and Jerusalem.

PRACTICE IN WRITING SCRIPT

So far, you have made all of your Hebrew letters in block form. But there is another form for the Hebrew alphabet, too. When people write to one another in the Hebrew language, they usually use a form of script writing which we call *cursive.* In the next few pages you can practice drawing Hebrew in cursive letters. So that the new cursive form will not be strange to you, copy the chart on the following page into your Hebrew notebook and refer to it as you practice the art of writing in Hebrew.

אָלֶף בֵּית

HEBREW ALPHABET

מ	מ	M	
ם	ם	Final M	
נ	נ	N	
ן	ן	Final N	
ס	ס	S	
ע	ע	Silent	
פ	פּ	P	
פ	פ	F	
ף	ף	Final F	
צ	צ	TS	
ץ	ץ	Final TS	
ק	ק	K	
ר	ר	R	
ש	שׁ	SH	
ש	שׂ	S	
ת	תּ	T	
ת	ת	T	

א	אַ	Silent	
ב	בּ	B	
ב	ב	V	
ג	גּ	(get) G	
ד	דּ	D	
ה	הַ	H	
ו	וֹ	V	
ז	זַ	Z	
ח	חַ	CH	
ט	טַ	T	
י	יִ	Y	
כ	כּ	K	
כ	כ	CH	
ך	ך	Final H	
ל	ל	L	

Note: In writing, begin each letter where you see the number 1. Then follow the arrows.

יוֹסֵף
עוּגָה
יָרֵחַ
שֶׁמֶשׁ
פִּיוֹן
כּוֹבַע
שׁוֹפָר
אֹהֶל
תַּרְנְגוֹל

עַיִן
בֵּיצָה
אָרוֹן
עִפָּרוֹן
עֵץ
בַּיִת
גָּמָל
פִּי
יָד

שָׁבַר

כִּסֵּא

נֵרוֹת

יְרָקוֹת

פֶּה

לֵב

מְלוּכָה

מֶלֶךְ

סֵפֶר

Printed in the USA
CPSIA information can be obtained
at www.ICGtesting.com
JSHW061916210224
57798JS00005B/12

9 780874 41216